— *the* —
BIRTH AND FIRST YEARS
OF JESUS THE MESSIAH

The Original Christmas Story

AUTHORIZED SELECTION FROM

THE COMMON GOSPEL

A Unified Biblical Account of the Times & Teachings
of Jesus the Messiah

MATTHEW, MARK, LUKE & JOHN

R. M. Mebane, Editor

Published by
Wordsmith Associates

The Four Evangelists (Matthew, Mark, Luke & John)

The Birth and First Years of Jesus the Messiah – The Original Christmas Story

R. M. MEBANE, Editor

Geneva, Illinois / Wordsmith Associates / 2021

24 pp / ISBN 978-0-9908547-1-5

BISAC Subject Codes:

BIB000000	*Bibles: General*
REL070000	*Religion: Christianity - General*
REL006160	*Religion: Biblical Reference - General*

An Authorized Selection from:

The Common Gospel – The Ultimate Testament to Jesus the Messiah

MILLENNIUM READER'S EDITION, 2018 Update

ISBN 978-0-9759290-4-9

25   24   23   22   10 9 8 7 6 5 4 3 2

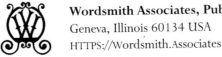

Wordsmith Associates, Publisher
Geneva, Illinois 60134 USA
HTTPS://Wordsmith.Associates

The Beginning of the Good News
of Jesus the Messiah, Son of God

Since many have undertaken to set a narrative in order
concerning those matters that have been fulfilled among us
— just as those who were eyewitnesses and servants of
the Word from the beginning delivered them to us — it
seemed good also, having traced the course of all things
accurately from the first, to compose an account so that
these things are known with certainty. It is written so that
you may believe that Jesus is the Son of God and that,
believing, you may have life in his name.

— the —

BIRTH AND FIRST YEARS OF JESUS THE MESSIAH

CONTENTS

Map of the Region
Foreword – *Eternal Word*

Afterword – *Come to the Light*

Map of the Region

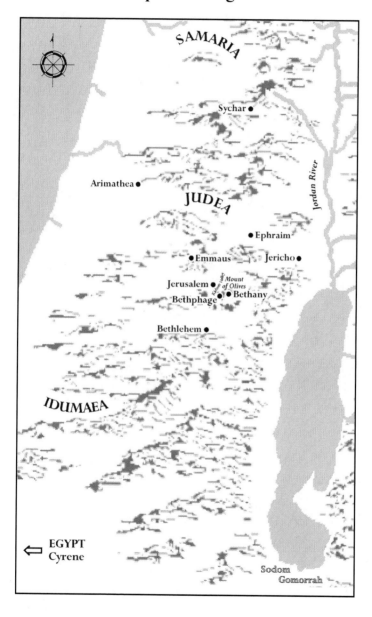

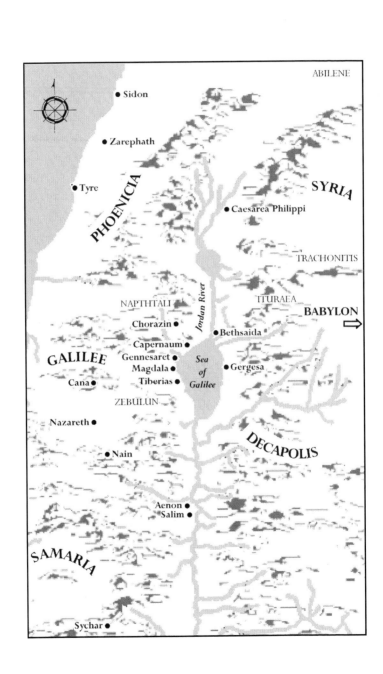

FOREWORD
Eternal Word

IN THE BEGINNING WAS the Word, and the Word was with God, and the Word was God.

He was in the beginning with God. All things were made through him, and nothing has been made without him. In him was life, and the life was the light of all people.

The light shines in the darkness, and the darkness has not overcome it.

⁂

The Word became flesh and lived among us. We saw his glory, such glory as of the one and only Son of the Father, full of grace and truth. From his fullness we have all received grace upon grace.

The law was given through Moses, but grace and truth came through Jesus the Messiah. No one has seen God at any time. The one and only Son, who is in the bosom of the Father, has declared him.

⁂

He was in the world, and the world was made through him, yet the world did not recognize him. He came to his own, and those who were his own did not receive him.

But to as many as received him, to those who believed in his name, he gave the right to become God's children, born not of blood, nor of the will of the flesh, nor of the will of man, but of God.

— *the* —
BIRTH AND FIRST YEARS
OF JESUS THE MESSIAH

An angel appears to Zacharias

IN THE DAYS OF Herod, the king of Judea, there was a certain priest named Zacharias, of the priestly division of Abijah. He had a wife of the daughters of Aaron, and her name was Elizabeth. They were both righteous before God, walking blamelessly in all the commandments and ordinances of the Lord. They lived in a Judean city in the hill country. But they had no child, because Elizabeth was barren, and they both were well advanced in years.

※

Now it happened, while Zacharias executed the priest's office before God in the order of his division according to the custom, his lot was to enter into the temple of the Lord and burn incense. As he did, an angel of the Lord appeared to him, standing on the right side of the altar of incense.

Zacharias was troubled when he saw him, and fear fell upon him. But the angel said,

Do not be afraid, Zacharias, because your request has been heard. Your wife, Elizabeth, will bear you a son, and you shall call him *John*. You will have joy and gladness. Even from his mother's womb, he will be filled with the Holy Spirit, and many will rejoice at his birth, for he will be great in the sight of the Lord.

In the spirit and power of Elijah, he will go before God to turn the hearts of parents to their children and the disobedient to the wisdom of the just, to make ready a people prepared for the Lord. He will turn many of the children of Israel to the Lord their God.

Zacharias doubted the angel. He said, "How can I be sure of this? I am an old man, and my wife is well advanced in years."

The angel answered him, "I am Gabriel, who stands in the presence of God. I was sent to speak to you and to bring you this good news. Behold, because you did not believe my words, which will be fulfilled in their proper time, you will not be able to speak. You will be silent until the day that these things happen."

The whole multitude of the people praying outside were waiting for Zacharias, and they marveled that he delayed in the temple.

When he came out, he could not speak to them. He continued making signs to them and remained mute.

They perceived that he had seen a vision in the temple.

⁓ᘝᘓᘗ⁓

When the days of Zacharias' service were fulfilled, he departed to his house and, after these days, his wife, Elizabeth, conceived.

She said, "Thus has the Lord done to me in the days in which he looked at me, to take away my reproach among men."

Elizabeth hid herself for five months.

An angel appears to Mary

One month after Elizabeth came out of seclusion, the angel Gabriel was sent from God to Nazareth, a city of Galilee, to a virgin named Mary.

Having come in, the angel said to her, "Rejoice, you highly favored one. The Lord is with you. Blessed are you among women."

Greatly troubled at these words, Mary considered what kind of salutation this might be. And the angel said to her,

Do not be afraid, Mary, for you have found favor with God. Behold, you will conceive in your womb and bring forth a son, and you will name him *Jesus.*

He will be great and will be called the Son of the Most High, and the Lord God will give him the throne of his father, David. He will reign over the house of Jacob forever. There will be no end to his kingdom.

Mary asked the angel, "How can this be, seeing that I am a virgin?"

The angel answered her, "Everything spoken by God is possible. Behold Elizabeth, your relative, in her old age and called barren, also has conceived a son. The Holy Spirit will come on you, and the power of the Most High will overshadow you. Therefore, the holy one who is born from you will also be called the Son of God."

Mary said, "Behold, I am the handmaid of the Lord. Let it be done to me according to your word."

Then the angel departed from her.

An angel appears to Joseph

When Mary was found to be pregnant by the Holy Spirit, she was pledged to be married to a man whose name was Joseph, of the house of David, but it was before they came together.

Joseph, being a righteous man and not willing to make her a public example, intended to put her away secretly. But while he thought about these things, behold, an angel of the Lord appeared to him in a dream, saying,

Do not be afraid, Joseph, son of David, to take Mary to yourself as your wife, for that which is conceived in her is of the Holy Spirit.

She shall bring forth a son, and you shall call his name *Jesus*, for it is he who shall save his people from their sins.

Joseph arose from his sleep and did as the angel of the Lord commanded him. He took Mary as his wife, but did not know her sexually until she had brought forth her firstborn son.

Mary visits Elizabeth

In those days, Mary went with haste into the hill country of Judea, to the house of Zacharias, where she stayed for about three months before returning to her home.

She entered into the house and greeted Elizabeth. Elizabeth was filled with the Holy Spirit and called out with a loud voice, "Blessed are you among women, and blessed is the fruit of your womb. For behold, when the voice of your greeting came into my ears, the baby leaped in my womb for joy. Why am I so favored, that the mother of my Lord should come to me? Blessed is she who believed, for there will be a fulfillment of the things which have been spoken to her from the Lord."

Mary said,

My soul magnifies the Lord. My spirit has rejoiced in God my savior, for he has looked at the humble state of his handmaid.

Behold, from now on, all generations will call me blessed, for he who is mighty has done great things for me. Holy is his name.

His mercy is for generations of generations on those who fear him. He has shown strength with his arm. He has scattered the proud in the imagination of their hearts. He has put down princes from their thrones and has exalted the lowly. He has filled the hungry with good things, and he has sent the rich away empty.

He has given help to his servant, Israel, so that mercy might be remembered as he spoke to our fathers, to Abraham, and to his seed forever.

John is born

Now the time that Elizabeth should give birth was fulfilled, and she brought forth a son. Her neighbors and her relatives heard that the Lord had magnified his mercy toward her, and they rejoiced with her.

On the eighth day, they came to circumcise the child, and they would have called him Zacharias, after the name of the father. But his mother said, "Not so, he will be called *John.*"

They said to her, "There is no one among your relatives who is called by this name." They made signs to his father to discover what he would have him called. They all marveled — Zacharias asked for a writing tablet, and wrote, "His name is *John.*"

Immediately, his mouth opened, his tongue was freed, and he spoke, blessing God.

Fear came on all who lived around them, and all these words were talked about throughout the hill country of Judea. The hand of the Lord was with this child, and all who heard these things laid them up in their heart, saying, "What then will this child be?"

His father, Zacharias, filled with the Holy Spirit, prophesied, saying,

> Blessed be the Lord, the God of Israel, for he has visited and worked redemption for his people. He has raised up a horn of salvation for us in the house of his servant David – salvation from our enemies and from the hand of all who hate us.
>
> So doing, he has shown mercy toward our forebears, reminding us of his holy covenant – the oath which he spoke to our father, Abraham – to grant that, being delivered out of the hand of our enemies, we should serve him without fear, in holiness and righteousness before him all the days of our life.
>
> And you, child, will be called a prophet of the Most High, for you will go before the face of the Lord to make ready his ways, to give knowledge of salvation to his people by the remission of their sins.
>
> From the tender mercy of our God, the dawn from on high will visit us – to shine on those who sit in darkness and the shadow of death, to guide our feet into the way of peace.

❧

The child grew. He never drank wine or strong drink, and he became strong in spirit. He was in the desert until the day of his public appearance to Israel.

Jesus the Messiah is born

Now the birth of Jesus the Messiah happened in this way.

A decree went out from Caesar Augustus that all the world should be enrolled. This was the first enrollment made when Quirinius was governor of Syria. All were to go to their own cities to enroll themselves.

Because Joseph was of the house and family of David, he went out from Galilee, from the city of Nazareth, into Judea, to the city of David, which is called Bethlehem. Joseph went to enroll himself with Mary, who was pregnant.

While they were there, the day came for her to give birth, and she brought forth her firstborn son.

She wrapped him in bands of cloth and, because there was no room for them in the inn, she laid him in a manger.

Shepherds seek the Child

In the same country, there were shepherds staying in the field, keeping watch by night over their flock, when an angel of the Lord came to stand by them, and the glory of the Lord shone around them.

They were terrified, but the angel said to them,

Do not be afraid, for, behold, I bring you good news of great joy, which will be to all the people. There is born to you, this day, in the city of David, a savior, who is the Messiah, the Lord.

This is the sign to you – you will find a baby wrapped in strips of cloth, lying in a manger.

Suddenly, a multitude of the heavenly host was there with the angel, praising God and saying,

Glory to God in the highest and, on earth, peace and good will toward all people.

When the angels went away from them into the sky, the shepherds said one to another, "Let us go to Bethlehem now and see this thing that has happened, which the Lord has made known to us."

They came with haste and found both Mary and Joseph, and the baby was lying in the manger.

When they saw it, they widely publicized the words spoken to them about this child. All who heard it wondered at these things, but Mary kept all these sayings, pondering them in her heart.

The shepherds returned, glorifying and praising God for all the things that they had heard and seen, just as it was told them.

The Holy Family visits Jerusalem

When eight days were fulfilled for the circumcision of the child, he was called *Jesus,* as was given by the angel before he was conceived in the womb.

When the days of their purification according to the law of Moses were fulfilled, Joseph and Mary brought him up to Jerusalem, to present him to the Lord, as it is written in the law of the Lord, "Every male who opens the womb shall be called holy to the Lord." They offered a sacrifice of two turtledoves according to that law.

꙳꙲꙲꙳

Behold, there was a man in Jerusalem whose name was Simeon. The Holy Spirit was on him, and he was righteous and devout, looking for the consolation of Israel. It had been revealed to him by the Holy Spirit that he should not see death before he had seen the Lord's Messiah.

He came in the Spirit into the temple. When the parents

brought in the child, Jesus, Simeon received him into his arms and blessed God and said,

> Master, you are now releasing your servant, according to your word, in peace. My eyes have seen your salvation, which you have prepared before the face of all peoples – a light for revelation to the nations and the glory of your people Israel.

Joseph and his mother were marveling at the things which were spoken concerning him.

Simeon blessed them and said to the mother, Mary,

> Behold, this child is set for the falling and the rising of many in Israel and for a sign which is spoken against. Yes, the thoughts of many hearts may be revealed, and a sword will pierce through your own soul.

※ ※ ※

There was also a prophetess, Anna, the daughter of Phanuel, of the tribe of Asher. She was of a great age, having lived with a husband seven years from her virginity, and she had been a widow for about eighty-four years. She did not depart from the temple, worshiping with fastings and petitions night and day.

At that very hour, she gave thanks to the Lord and spoke of him to all those who were looking for redemption in Jerusalem.

Magi seek the Child

Some time after Jesus was born in Bethlehem of Judea, behold, magi from the east came to Jerusalem, saying, "Where is he who is born King of the Jews? We saw his star in the east and have come to worship him."

※ ※ ※

When Herod the king heard it, he was troubled, and all Jerusalem was troubled with him.

Gathering together all the chief priests and scribes of the people, he asked them where the Messiah would be born.

They said to him, "In Bethlehem of Judea, for thus it is written through the prophet, 'You Bethlehem, land of Judah, are in no way least among the princes of Judah – for out of you shall come forth a governor, who shall shepherd my people, Israel.'"

Herod secretly called the magi and learned from them exactly what time the star appeared. Then he sent them to Bethlehem, and said, "Go and search diligently for the young child. When you have found him, bring me word, so that I also may come and worship him."

Having heard the king, the magi went their way and, behold, the star which they saw in the east stood over where the young child was.

When they saw the star, they rejoiced with exceedingly great joy. They came into the house and saw the young child with Mary, his mother, and they fell down and worshiped him. From among their treasures, they offered him gifts of gold, frankincense, and myrrh.

Warned in a dream that they should not return to Herod, they went back to their own country another way.

When Herod saw that he was mocked by the magi, he was exceedingly angry and sent out an order to kill all the male children who were in Bethlehem and in all the surrounding countryside, from two years old and under, according to the exact time which he had learned from the magi.

※❊※

The Holy Family departs for Egypt

After the magi had departed, behold, an angel of the Lord appeared to Joseph in a dream, saying,

Arise and take the young child and his mother, and flee into Egypt, and stay there until I tell you, for Herod will seek the young child to destroy him.

He arose and took the young child and his mother by night, and departed into Egypt and was there until the death of Herod.

※❊※

The Child grows

When Herod was dead, behold, an angel of the Lord appeared in a dream to Joseph in Egypt, saying,

Arise and take the young child and his mother, and go into the land of Israel, for those who sought the young child's life are dead.

He arose and took the young child and his mother, and came into the land of Israel. But, when he heard that Archelaus was reigning over Judea in the place of his father, Herod, he was afraid to go there. So they returned to the region of Galilee, to their own city, Nazareth. The child grew, became strong in spirit, filled with wisdom, and the grace of God was upon him.

Young Jesus learns

Every year his parents went to Jerusalem at the feast of the Passover with the boy Jesus and, when he was twelve years old, they went up to Jerusalem according to the custom of the feast.

When they had fulfilled the days, as they were returning, Jesus stayed behind in Jerusalem, but Joseph and his mother did not know it.

Supposing him to be in the company, they went a day's journey. They looked for him among their relatives and acquaintances and, when they did not find him, they returned to Jerusalem, looking for him.

After three days they found him in the temple, sitting in the midst of the teachers, both listening to them and asking them questions. All who heard him were amazed at his understanding.

When they saw him, they were astonished, and his mother said to him, "Son, why have you treated us this way? Behold, your father and I were anxiously looking for you."

He said to them, "Why were you looking for me? Did you not know that I must be in my Father's house?" They did not understand what he said to them.

☙❧

He went with them to Nazareth and was subject to them. His mother kept all these sayings in her heart.

And Jesus increased in wisdom and stature, in human favor and in favor with God.

AFTERWORD
Come to the Light

GOD SO LOVED THE world that he gave his one and only Son, so that whoever believes in him should not perish but have eternal life.

God did not send his Son into the world to judge the world but in order that the world should be saved through him.

Those who believe in him are not judged, but those who do not believe have been judged already, because they have not believed in the name of the one and only Son of God.

This is the judgment – that the light has come into the world, and people loved the darkness rather than the light, for their works were evil. Those who do evil hate the light and do not come to the light, lest their works be exposed.

But those who act in truth come to the light, so that their works may be revealed as having been done in God.

ABOUT THIS BOOK

The Birth and First Years of Jesus the Messiah presents the first part of the 16-part volume, *The Common Gospel*, which unites the Gospels according to Matthew, Mark, Luke & John and presents the times and teachings of Jesus in one common framework. The parts of *The Common Gospel* include:

The Common Gospel:
The Ultimate Testament to Jesus the Messiah
ISBN 978-0-9759290-4-9 / Paperback / 330 pages / ©2018

The Common Gospel combines the four traditional Gospels and presents the *Good News* of Jesus in a single, unified book. In so doing, it brings clarity and focus to the history of Jesus the Messiah as it assembles the original gospel fragments to frame a naturally flowing lifeline for the Son of Man — from his humble and holy birth through to his crowning glorification. The panoramic view that results is extraordinary and casts Jesus the Messiah in new and revealing light.

For additional information, please visit the publisher's website at:
HTTPS://Wordsmith.Associates
Or correspond via email to: PUBLISHER@ Wordsmith.Associates

Made in the USA
Columbia, SC
25 September 2022

67922136R00015